Table of Contents

SERIES EDITOR Thomas S. C. Farrell

REVISED EDITION

Teaching Grammar

William J. Crawford

www.tesol.org/bookstore

TESOL International Association
1925 Ballenger Avenue
Alexandria, Virginia, 22314 USA
www.tesol.org

Director of Publishing and Product Development: Myrna Jacobs
Copy Editor: Meg Moss
Production Editor: Kari S. Dalton
Cover Design: Citrine Sky Design
Interior Design and Layout: Capitol Communications, LLC
Printing: Gasch Printing, LLC

ISBN 9781945351822
eBook ISBN 9781945351839
Library of Congress Control Number 2019956817

Series Editor's Preface

The *English Language Teacher (ELTD)* series consists of a set of short resource books for ESL/EFL teachers that are written in a jargon-free and accessible manner for all types of teachers of English (native, nonnative, experienced, and novice). The ELTD series is designed to offer teachers a theory-to-practice approach to second language teaching, and each book presents a wide variety of practical approaches to and methods of teaching the topic at hand. Each book also offers reflections to help teachers interact with the materials presented. The books can be used in preservice settings or in in-service courses and by individuals looking for ways to refresh their practice. Now, after nearly 10 years in print, the ELTD series presents newly updated, revised editions that are even more dynamic than their first editions. Each of these revised books has an expanded number of chapters, as well as updated references from which various activities have been drawn and lesson plans for teachers to consider.

William Crawford's revised edition of *Teaching Grammar* again explores different approaches to how teachers can teach grammar in second language classrooms. He has added a chapter on designing writing assignments, updated the references and research, and added more reflective questions as well as new activities throughout the book, as well as detailed guidelines of teaching grammar with sample activities that teachers can consider. This revised edition is again a valuable addition to the literature in our profession.

I am very grateful to the authors of the ELTD series for sharing their knowledge and expertise with other TESOL professionals to make these short books affordable for all language teachers throughout the world. It is truly an honor for me to work again with each of these authors for the advancement of TESOL.

Thomas S. C. Farrell

CHAPTER 1

Introduction

Teaching grammar is, in some ways, very different from teaching reading, writing, speaking, and listening. The most obvious reason for this is that grammar is an important component in all language skills. In any language, using language without some knowledge of how words combine to form larger units of language is nearly impossible. Lacking such knowledge makes interacting with other people, giving a presentation, reading a book or article, or writing an essay very difficult. From this perspective, both receptive (reading, listening) and productive (speaking, listening) skills depend on knowledge of grammar.

One important concept in grammar and grammar teaching is understanding the difference between two aspects of grammar knowledge: the ability to explain a grammar concept (explicit knowledge) and the ability to use grammar appropriately (implicit knowledge). These two concepts are not as closely related as one may think, and researchers debate extensively the relationship between these two types of knowledge (Ellis et al., 2009), especially when it comes to teaching and learning a second language. In some situations, grammar teaching may require an explanation of rules— a clear way of presenting how words fit together in some ways but not in others. For example, to explain why *eat it up* is preferred over *eat up it*, some teachers may describe the different types of multiword verbs and provide rules (or even lists to memorize) of multiword verbs; other teachers may not be able to explain why *eat up it* sounds strange or may not even think an explanation is worth providing. Regardless of the perspective of different teachers, the majority of grammar teachers would agree that they would prefer that their students produce *eat it up* and not *eat up it*, which illustrates the idea that teachers may not have the same approach to teaching grammar but would likely agree on the outcome of grammar teaching—appropriate use and understanding of grammar. Thinking about grammar teaching from this perspective illustrates that teachers may have varying degrees of knowledge about how to describe grammar explicitly, but a high degree of explicit knowledge does not automatically result in accurate and appropriate language use. In addition to the various types of grammar knowledge is the issue of how to teach; that is, how to sequence classroom activities, how to decide what to teach and when to teach it, how to respond to student questions, and how to make lessons interesting and engaging for students.

In fact, grammar teaching consists of two different types of knowledge: teacher knowledge and teaching knowledge. From a teacher knowledge perspective, teachers need to know how to explain grammar. *Teacher knowledge* involves knowing something about relative clauses, subject–verb agreement, comparative constructions, modal verbs, tense, and many other aspects of grammar. *Teaching knowledge* relates to the techniques and approaches that help students use grammar effectively (appropriately and accurately) and effortlessly (so that students can be free to address other considerations). Successful grammar teachers have some level of comfort with both teacher knowledge and teaching knowledge.

Additionally, effective teaching relates to confidence. Obviously, teaching experience contributes to confidence as does an interest in subject matter and a belief in the curriculum. One way to gain such confidence in teaching is through reflective practice, which provides teachers with an opportunity to understand those aspects of their own teaching that seem most relevant to them at a given time. Reflective practice allows teachers to identify, describe, and understand their beliefs about teaching and therefore to make aspects of their teaching explicit in ways that can inform their future teaching practices. The reflective questions in this book are intended to help teachers gain explicit knowledge of different aspects of grammar which, in turn, can lead to more effective grammar teaching. Whatever approach one uses in the teaching of grammar, it is nearly always better to teach things that can be clearly explained and understood. Whether teachers choose to use such explicit knowledge in their pedagogical approaches is a matter of context, teaching style, or curricular goals; however, knowing why things are the way they are (teacher knowledge) is surely an important component of being an effective teacher.

This book uses reflective practice to help grammar teachers become better by addressing both their teacher knowledge and their teaching knowledge of grammar. The following chapters define grammar from a teacher perspective (chapter 2); show how corpus linguistics can be a useful tool for grammar teachers (chapter 3); cover some basic concepts of grammar teaching found in research (chapter 4); and address important considerations and components of teaching grammar (chapter 5).

Grammar: Form, Meaning, and Use

The concept of grammar and how to teach it includes a wide range of perspectives. Some teaching approaches focus on formal rules of grammar that precede language practice or performance. This *deductive* approach to the teaching of grammar provides a general rule and then gives students opportunities to practice the language using specific examples. Other approaches provide students with examples of language and ask them to state the grammar rules that apply. This *inductive* approach expects students to discover the grammar rule by reference to the examples. A good deal of research has been undertaken in the differences and effectiveness of inductive and deductive approaches to teaching grammar (Ellis, 2002) that shows the effectiveness of both approaches in different contexts and with different types of grammar rules. Of course, within the inductive/deductive dichotomy of teaching grammar, a variety of different techniques can be used, which suggests that adopting a single approach to grammar teaching does not account for many relevant factors such as the various reasons and purposes for learning English, the contexts in which it is learned, the age of students, the class size, the relative difficulty of the grammar feature in question, and the proficiency level of students. Thus, ensuring that student needs are being met requires a wide range of approaches and techniques in grammar teaching. To meet these needs, a very basic question must first be answered: what is the main purpose of grammar teaching?

The perspective adopted in this book is that grammar teaching in L2 contexts seeks to help learners gain grammar ability so that they can use grammar accurately, meaningfully, and appropriately. These three adjectives that define grammar ability—*accurate*, *meaningful*, and *appropriate*—may be quite different from other teachers' views of grammar. Reflection, however, reveals that grammar knowledge does not just relate to accuracy. Relevant components of meaning (semantics) and use (pragmatics) are important parts of grammar knowledge. Knowing the distinctions between these components of grammar knowledge can help grammar teachers be more effective.

Form, Meaning, and Use

One useful way to think about grammar is through a form, meaning, and use (FMU) perspective made popular by *The Grammar Book* (Celce-Murcia & Larsen-Freeman, 2015), as well as Diane Larsen-Freeman's book *Teaching Language: From grammar to grammaring* (2003). Each of these components are discussed in more detail ahead.

Form refers to the structure of a phrase or clause. In a given context, certain forms are required in English to be considered accurate. Form describes either the required form of a word (*She <u>likes</u> to travel* is preferred to *She <u>like</u> to travel*) or a required word order (*I can't tell you* is preferred to *I no can tell you*). Form is often described by reference to rules that speakers follow (either consciously or unconsciously) and is likely what most people think of when they think of grammar.

REFLECTIVE QUESTION

- Thinking about your own understanding of English grammar, would you characterize your grammar knowledge as mostly explicit, mostly implicit, or a combination of both explicit and implicit?

Grammar ability involves not just explicitly learning or describing rules but also using language for real communicative purposes. Of course, rules provide helpful guidelines for understanding grammar and clearly have their place in the grammar classroom, but being able to state a grammar rule does not mean that one can actually use it. The distinction between stating a grammar rule and using grammar suggests that one type of knowledge (explicit knowledge) does not necessarily translate into another type of knowledge (implicit knowledge). The curriculum designer or teacher must ultimately decide to determine the extent to which the class addresses formal rule-learning, but all teachers and curriculum designers should be aware that grammar does not consist entirely of formal rule-learning.

In addition to form, grammar contains a semantic (*meaning*) component. In fact, if people paid no attention to meaning, what would be the point of communication? If grammar teachers only focus on form, they quickly run into problems. For example, *I saw a movie* means something very different from *I am seeing a movie*. A learner may produce either structure accurately (the forms of both sentences are accurate), but the two sentences have very different intended meanings. Thus, learners need to know how to use the correct structure to reach an intended meaning.

REFLECTIVE QUESTION

● What other examples of meaning distinctions in grammar might cause confusion?

Moreover, certain types of grammar forms are preferable over others, depending on the context. For example, sentences with contractions (*I'm happy to see you're here*) are much more common in spoken language or informal types of writing than in written academic contexts. Common distinctions such as conversation versus writing or formal versus informal illustrate systematic differences in how grammar is used in the two contexts. When teachers caution their students, "Don't talk like you write" or "You wouldn't say that in a formal presentation," they are talking about *use*. The relationship between grammar and context is found in research on *register variation* (Biber, 1988, and Biber & Conrad, 2019). Research in this area is based on the idea that the form of language depends on the contexts in which it is used. Register analysis shows systematic differences between grammar form in contexts such as conversation, academic writing, news writing, and fiction. *The Longman Grammar of Spoken and Written English,* or LGSWE (Biber et al., 1999), provides a comprehensive description of grammar from a use perspective. The next chapter looks at register variation in more detail.

One useful way to consider form, meaning, and use is by examining how these different perspectives can describe a single grammar feature. Table 2.1 provides a description of how reference to form, meaning, and use can describe two different features of grammar.

Table 2.1. Form, Meaning, and Use of Phrasal Verbs and Present Progressive

Grammar feature	Form	Meaning	Use
Phrasal verbs	A multiword verb that ● Consists of a lexical verb and a particle (e.g., *give up*) ● Has particle movement (*give up the idea; give the idea up*)	● Can often be substituted with a single verb (e.g., *surrender*)	● Used most in spoken language; frequent in fiction; rare in academic registers ● More common in less formal contexts
Present progressive	Auxiliary verb *be* + gerund: ● *She is reading on her own these days.* Different from semi-modal: ● *Larry is going to see if he can come.*	● Expresses an ongoing or continuous action in present time	● More frequent in conversation than writing ● Used primarily with dynamic verbs (*go, run, walk*) than stative verbs (*know, love*) or copular verbs (*seem, appear*)

As seen in Table 2.1, any given grammar feature can be described from three perspectives. Phrasal verbs, for example, consist of a lexical verb and a particle. They also allow for movement of objects (particularly when the object is a pronoun) to reside between the verb and its particle. From a meaning perspective, phrasal verbs often have single word synonyms. From a use perspective, they are more common in spoken, informal contexts than in written formal contexts, but this is not to say that formal academic writing does not contain phrasal verbs. The present progressive form requires a gerund to follow the auxiliary verb *be*. Progressive aspect is used to show that an action is ongoing. Progressive verbs are also more frequent in conversation as opposed to writing and tend to occur with specific semantic classes of verbs. Describing grammar features as in Table 2.1 has a number of advantages over focusing solely on form, meaning, or use separately.

First, some teachers may have explicit knowledge of certain pieces of a grammar feature but may not have explicit knowledge of all three aspects. For example, a teacher may be very comfortable explaining how to form the present progressive but may not be able to explain how to use it in authentic discourse. Teachers with explicit knowledge of all three aspects of a given grammar feature are better equipped to explain a given feature to students and to devise activities that raise students' awareness of grammar.

Second, viewing grammar from an FMU perspective shows that knowing grammar does not just mean knowing rules (and exceptions to rules); it involves knowing how to use form to gain an intended meaning in a given context. Furthermore, FMU can guide teachers in their selection of grammar features to teach. Consider these two examples:

1. Speaker A: *What does she like to do?* Speaker B: *She like to travel.*

2. Speaker A: *What did you do last night?* Speaker B: *I am seeing a movie.*

In both examples 1 and 2, speaker B makes a grammar mistake. In 1B, the subject of the sentence (*she*) should agree with the verb (third-person singular subjects require verbs in different forms than other types of subjects). By contrast, in 2B uses the incorrect tense and aspect and expresses an incorrect meaning. So, what do these examples illustrate? Grammar errors that result in meaning confusion (example 2) are likely more worthy of a teacher's focus than those that are purely formal (example 1). Additionally, understanding the nature of the errors that students may make may help teachers: a form-based error in example 1 does not affect meaning and may be more frequent and persistent exactly for that reason; a meaning-based error such as the one in example 2 perhaps merits closer attention because it interferes with meaning. Of course, this does not necessarily mean that teachers should pay no attention to form-type errors, but it does illustrate that the FMU distinction is a useful guide to help teachers decide the focus of their lessons as well as how to describe and explain grammar to students.

Finally, providing such descriptions can serve as an impetus for students to be active participants in their own learning and understanding of grammar. Raising awareness not only of form and meaning aspects of grammar but also of grammar use allows students to be active consumers of different types of grammar knowledge and may even help them to notice how grammar is used in different contexts and promote their active participation in their own grammar learning. As discussed in Larsen-Freeman (2003), engaging students in the three goals of grammar teaching—accuracy, meaningfulness, and appropriacy—can be achieved by raising their awareness of the components of grammar knowledge—form, meaning, and use—and foster dynamic involvement for students to engage in grammar learning in some of the same ways that students can be engaged in learning reading, writing, speaking, and listening. In fact, Larsen-Freeman encourages this type of participation in grammar learning by coining the term "grammaring" as a "fifth skill [that] is intimately interconnected with the other skills" (Larsen-Freeman, 2003, p. 143).

REFLECTIVE QUESTIONS

● In what ways can the goals of accuracy, meaningfulness, and appropriateness and the components of form, meaning, and use relate to how the learning of grammar can be seen as a skill? Is "grammaring" a fifth skill?

CHAPTER 3

Form, Meaning, Use, and Corpora

As discussed in chapter 2, the goals of using grammar in accurate, appropriate, and meaningful ways is supported by an FMU perspective on grammar, which helps both teachers and students view grammar as more than just formal rule knowledge. To describe grammar from this perspective, though, requires sources of information that are reliable, authentic, and go beyond simple rule descriptions. A reliable source of information provides a fair representation of language and shows how a specific grammar feature is used. Sometimes, an intuition of how language is used is incorrect. Authentic sources of language are also needed because they reflect language as it is actually used. Teachers may want to adapt authentic materials to make them more understandable to students, but knowing how grammar is used in real-life situations provides the type of information that is likely to be more helpful for students because they will be using language in these same situations. As for going beyond simple rule description, all language (including grammar) is complex and subject to variation. Raising the awareness of such variability in both teachers and students can help them both to be active participants in the understanding and control over grammar with the ultimate goal of helping students become better at "grammaring" as discussed in the previous chapter.

This chapter shows how one approach to language description—*corpus linguistics*—provides reliable and authentic examples that teachers can use to inform their understanding of grammar. A *corpus* is a collection of texts related to a specific situation of language use (e.g., spoken language, written language, or academic lectures). Most often, computers are used to identify the form, meaning, and use of a given grammar feature. The type of information provided by corpora allows insights into grammar that are not possible in descriptions that do not use corpora. After a short description of corpus linguistics, some examples of corpus-based grammar description are provided. The primary goal of this chapter is to encourage teachers to use corpus information to inform their own understanding of grammar so that they can become better grammar teachers. A secondary goal is to raise teachers' awareness of how corpora can be used to describe grammar in situations where they may want to expose students to corpus examples during grammar instruction. This issue will be raised in more detail in the following chapter.

Corpus Linguistics

Corpus linguistics is a method of investigating language by reference to large amounts of language that occur in specific contexts. Scholars use corpus description to gain new insights into areas such as language change and variation, sociolinguistics, lexicology, and stylistics (McEnery, Xiao, & Tono, 2006, for a good description of corpus linguistics and the various ways that corpora have been used in applied linguistics). The impact also extends to language teaching and learning. Series of corpus-based textbooks (e.g., Reppen, 2012; McCarthy, McCarten, & Sandiford, 2005) provide teachers and learners with authentic examples of language as opposed to contrived materials often found in more traditional textbooks.

In addition to language-learning materials, corpus-based descriptive grammars such as the *Longman Grammar of Spoken and Written English* (*LGSWE*) can also be used to enhance understanding of grammar and to guide teaching decisions. Corpora can reveal information about language that may have previously gone unnoticed (such as the fact that simple aspect occurs more frequently than progressive aspect in spoken language). Corpora can also illustrate the relationship between a grammar structure and specific words. For example, the most common verb to head an *–ing* clause in conversation is *keep* (*I keep telling you that*). Corpus data readily reveals frequency information to help teachers focus on aspects of language that students are most likely to encounter in a given context.

Along with corpus-based textbooks and descriptions, teachers can use corpora themselves to learn more about a specific grammar feature. This chapter looks at three grammar features described in the LGSWE (multiword verbs, tense, and aspect) and one feature (verbs followed by gerunds and infinitives) in the *Corpus of Contemporary American English* (COCA). Finally, a more recent grammatical phenomenon—lexical bundles—as described in both the LGSWE and the COCA, are discussed.

REFLECTIVE QUESTION

- What are some advantages of describing grammar from an FMU perspective through the use of corpora?

Multiword Verbs

It would be difficult to find a learner who has not struggled with multiword verbs in English. One problematic aspect concerns meaning. If someone *carries out an experiment,* no actual transport (*carries*) or direction (*out*) is involved. Thus, students must learn specific meanings associated with specific multiword verbs. This problem is further complicated when the meaning of a multiword verb changes depending on the context. That is to say, *look up* means one thing in *I looked up the address* and something quite different in *I looked up the street.*

Another source of difficulty is found in the variation that is permissible in some constructions (*I looked up the address/I looked the address up*) but not in others (*I looked up the street/*I looked the street up*). In the first example, both constructions are grammatical, but in the second example, the second construction is not (hence the asterisk next to the sentence).

REFLECTIVE QUESTION

- What do you know about multiword verbs? How would you describe the difference between *I looked up the address* and *I looked the address up*?

According to the LGSWE, multiword verbs come in two major types: phrasal verbs and prepositional verbs. The major distinguishing factor between phrasal and prepositional verbs is that transitive phrasal verbs allow the verb to be separated (*I looked up the address/I looked the address up*). The separation is required when the object is a pronoun (**I looked up it/ I looked it up*). The second type of multiword verb is sometimes called a prepositional verb, and it does not allow separation between the two parts (*I looked at the painting/*I looked the painting at*). In addition to phrasal and prepositional verbs are single-word verbs followed by prepositions, such as *I went into the store.*

The form information provided here is not specific to corpus descriptions. Most grammar books that cover multiword verbs include a discussion similar to this one. But beyond this, more traditional grammar books may not present any criteria for choosing which multiword verbs to address in instruction. Some books may just provide lists in alphabetical order or rely on the author's intuition regarding the most important multiword verbs to include. Corpora, on the other hand, can provide frequency information to guide teachers in their decisions about which multiword verbs to teach.

The LGSWE says that the most common phrasal verbs in English are intransitive (*come on* and *go on*); the most common transitive phrasal verbs are *get in*, *pick up*, and *find out*. The most common prepositional verb is *look at*; other common phrasal verbs are *say to*, *listen to*, and *talk to*. Furthermore, the majority of phrasal verbs (whether transitive or intransitive) describe activities (*move in*, *pull up/down*, *turn on*, *wake up*). Although common prepositional verbs also describe activities (*look at*, *go through*), they also commonly describe communication (*say to*) and mental conditions (*think of* and *think about*).

Phrasal verbs are most common in fiction writing and conversation and less common in newspapers and academic writing. The most common phrasal verbs in conversation, fiction, newspapers, and academic writing (occurring more than 100 times per million words) are found in Table 3.1.

REFLECTIVE QUESTION

- How might corpus information about multiword verbs be helpful for you?

Teaching Grammar

Tense and Aspect in English

The *tense* and *aspect* system of English presents another area of difficulty for students. Verbs change their form depending on whether they are in present or past tense or whether they are in simple, progressive, perfect, or perfect progressive aspect. Tense and aspect also combine to give both present and past perfect, progressive, or perfect progressive.

Corpus description shows that certain verbs are more or less likely to occur in the present or past tense. For example, verbs such as *bet*, *doubt*, *know*, and *suppose* are found in the present tense more than 80% of the time; conversely, verbs such as *reply*, *remark*, *smile*, and *whisper* occur in the past tense more than 80% of the time. Present-tense verbs usually describe mental or logical states, and past-tense verbs usually describe human activity (often related to speaking). Furthermore, although present-tense verbs are more common than past-tense verbs overall, there are register distinctions worthy of mention. Conversation and academic registers are much more likely to contain verbs in the present tense; fiction is much more likely to contain verbs in the past tense, and newspapers use both past and present equally.

Table 3.1. Common Phrasal Verbs Across Registers

Conversation	Fiction	Newspapers	Academic writing
come on, go on, get up, get in, find out	come on, get up, sit down, go on, stand up, pick up, look up	go on, carry out	carry out

REFLECTIVE QUESTION

● How might corpus information concerning tense be useful for you?

The verbs *know* and *reply* can occur in the present or past tense, but students are far more likely to encounter the verb *know* in the present tense and the verb *reply* in the past tense. Teachers can use this type of information to link tense with specific verb meanings, and they can also use it in activities where students are learning tense distinctions as they are exposed to verbs that they are likely to encounter in their respective tenses. This same idea extends to aspect.

The LGSWE shows that simple aspect is by far the most common aspect used in English. When verbs are marked for aspect, they fall into specific semantic categories. Common verbs in perfect aspect are *been, had, got, gone, done, made,* and *shown.* In progressive aspect, common verbs fall into two categories: activity/physical state verbs (*bleed, chase, shop, starve*) and communication verbs (*chat, joke, kid, moan*).

Furthermore, although simple aspect is much more common than progressive and perfect aspect (90% of all verbs are in simple aspect across all registers), perfect aspect is more common than progressive aspect.

Gerund and Infinitive Complements

REFLECTIVE QUESTION

● How might the information on aspect be helpful for you?

In addition to corpus-based descriptions such as the LGSWE, teachers can also use existing corpora to learn about grammar. One of the most readily available and easiest to use is the COCA, constructed by Mark Davies and available at http://corpus.byu.edu/. COCA is one of seven corpora currently available on this site. Others include the *British National Corpus* and the *TIME Magazine Corpus of American English.* All of the corpora use the same search procedures, so once teachers learn to use the search tools, they can search any of the available corpora. The search tools in the left column of the display also contain links to helpful directions that take the user through a step-by-step process for using all of the tools. Becoming proficient in using the search tools may take time, but once teachers are, the possibilities are endless.

For example, what the COCA says about common verbs followed by gerunds and infinitives demonstrates the power of this corpus. Verbs in English vary in whether they take an infinitive clause (*She told me to open the door*) or a clause containing a gerund (*She enjoys watching sports*). The verb determines the form of the clause; one cannot say *She told me opening the door* or *She enjoys to watch sports*.

Verbs such as *tell* and *enjoy* differ from a verb such as *begin*, where both a gerund and an infinitive are possible (*It began to rain/It began raining*). A more traditional treatment provides students with lists of verbs that fall into one of the three categories. For those in the final category, practice may involve using the verb with both a gerund and an infinitive. Although certain verbs can take either complement type, what does the corpus say? By way of example, three verbs that take either gerund or infinitive complements—*begin*, *start*, and *continue*—will be the focus. These three verbs vary in their preference for complement types.

As seen in Table 3.2, the verbs *begin* and *continue* take infinitive complements more frequently, and *start* takes gerund complements more frequently. The verb *begin* is more than twice as likely to be followed by an infinitive complement than a gerund complement; *start* is more than one and a half times more likely to take a gerund complement; and *continue* is nearly nine times more likely to take an infinitive complement. When covering this specific grammar point, this type of information can aid teachers in their ability to explain the preference for complement types as well as to help students by exposing them not to what is possible but instead to the forms they are most likely to encounter.

Table 3.2. Gerund and Infinitive Complements of Begin, Start, and Continue

Verb	Gerund	Infinitive
begin	85	180
start	134	84
continue	15	132

Note: Values are per million words.

In addition to gerund and infinitive complements, COCA can also demonstrate what sorts of verbs are found in the complements of each type. For example, Table 3.3 shows the different verbs in gerund complements for all three verbs. COCA can easily show teachers and students useful information about common and preferred collocations (for example, *start talking* is more common than *begin talking*) that can be used as examples in both explanation and grammar activities.

Table 3.3. Common Verbs with Gerund Complements

Verb	Gerund complement
begin	*working, taking, making, looking, using*
start	*talking, looking, thinking, getting, making*
continue	*working, doing, talking, using, playing*

REFLECTIVE QUESTION

● If you were teaching complement types using these three verbs, how would you use this information to help?

Lexical Bundles

A final grammar point considered in this chapter relates to a relatively new phenomenon that is a frequent topic among corpus researchers—*lexical bundles* (also known as *n-grams*). Lexical bundles are common combinations of words, and, although they may not traditionally be included in grammar textbooks, one could argue that they belong in the realm of grammar instruction.

Lexical bundles differ from other multiword chunks of language, such as multiword verbs or the so-called frozen expressions that do not always have a literal meaning (*bare your soul* or *in the bag*). Lexical bundles (also referred to as *n-grams* because researchers can look at two, three, four, five, or more word sequences) are not defined by their reference to meaning but instead by their common occurrence in a given register of language. The frequency of lexical bundles is not trivial. In fact, the LGSWE has found that phrasal-prepositional verbs along with three- and four-word lexical bundles make up 30% of all words in conversation and 21% of all words in academic writing. So why would they be considered relevant in grammar instruction?

In an influential article looking at lexical bundles in a corpus of registers of university language (e.g., textbooks, academic writing, lectures), Biber, Conrad, and Cortes (2004) extended the analysis of lexical bundles first discussed in the LGSWE and found that four-word lexical bundles have certain characteristics that suggest they have a grammatical status. Evidence for this position is found in the FMU view of grammar discussed in chapter 2.

From the perspective of form, many lexical bundles include parts of grammar categories such as verb phrases (*you don't have to*), clauses (*I don't know if*), noun phrases (*the back of the*), and prepositional phrases (*a little bit about*). Most traditional approaches to grammar instruction would not consider these worthy of teaching because they do not consist of a whole phrase or clause. The term *constituent* is often used to refer to complete structural units such as noun phrases (*the back of the book*) or clauses (*although you may not know this . . .*), and most grammar books focus on phrases and clauses as relevant structures. But if, as shown by corpus evidence, many frequent chunks of language do not form a constituent, then it is necessary to be open to the possibility that these fragments of phrases and clauses play an important role in grammar.

A second characteristic of lexical bundles relates to how they serve a function in language. They can express the stance of a speaker or writer (*are more likely to*), organize discourse by introducing a topic (*I would like to)*, and refer to things or concepts (*that's one of the*). Lexical bundles have meanings associated with them.

In addition to clear meaning differences, Biber, Conrad, and Cortes (2004) show that lexical bundles in textbooks and academic writing are more likely to take the form of noun phrase bundles, but classroom teaching includes a fairly equal distribution of noun phrase, verb phrase, and clausal types. The differences are not only structural: this study found that textbooks and academic writing also includes more referential bundles than does classroom teaching, where referential and stance bundles are equally distributed. Thus, lexical bundles vary in different contexts.

Even though the vast majority of grammar textbooks do not cover them, lexical bundles seem to have a grammar status from an FMU perspective. The LGSWE devotes an entire chapter to lexical bundles. More recently, Mark Davies's corpus site (http://www.ngrams.info/) offers a downloadable list of the most frequent two-, three-, four-, and five-word n-grams in

COCA. Table 3.4 provides some frequent lexical bundles in conversation and academic writing taken from Biber, Conrad, and Cortes (2004). All of the bundles in the table occur more than 100 times per million words in their respective registers.

Frequent lexical bundles can be used in many helpful ways to teach grammar. One possibility is to ask students to write sentences using lexical bundles (see chapter 5 for an example of this). Another possibility is to have them look at examples of different lexical bundles in context and try to determine whether a specific meaning or function is associated with them.

Table 3.4. Frequent Four-Word Lexical Bundles in Four Registers

Conversation	Classroom teaching	Academic prose	Textbooks
I don't know what	if you want to	on the other hand	at the end of
I don't want to	I want you to	in the case of	
do you want to	is going to be		
I was going to	to be able to		
are you going to			
one of the things			
of the things that			

Source: Biber, Conrad, and Cortes (2004)

REFLECTIVE QUESTIONS

- Do you see lexical bundles as more closely related to grammar or to vocabulary?

- How might you address lexical bundles in a grammar class?

This chapter has shown how corpora can provide helpful information for grammar teachers. Reflective questions in this chapter have asked you to consider how corpus information would be useful in your teaching.

Although corpora can likely be used in many different ways, using a good corpus-based reference book or using a corpus itself will inform both teacher knowledge of grammar (by providing clear descriptions of FMU) and teaching knowledge (by helping teachers choose what features or aspects of features to address in their teaching).

FMU information obtained from corpora can be used to complement descriptions in virtually any grammar teaching material. That is, corpus information need not replace textbooks or worksheets, but information taken from corpora can provide excellent examples of preferred choices or frequently occurring collocations. Nevertheless, it is not always possible to use a corpus to search for all grammar structures. Some grammar structures, such as relative clauses, can be difficult to find using the existing search tools. For more complex grammar structures, a good corpus-based reference book would be a better choice. But for many other grammar features, publicly available corpora can provide readily accessible and useful information for teachers and students.

REFLECTIVE QUESTIONS

- Corpus information often makes reference to frequency. How might frequency relate to grammar teaching?

- What are some limitations of corpora and corpus-based research?

CHAPTER 4

Grammar Teaching and Grammar Knowledge

This chapter covers two issues related to grammar teaching: (1) the role of grammar teaching and research that supports form-focused instruction and (2) different types of grammar knowledge (implicit and explicit knowledge). With respect to the first point, teachers should be aware of why grammar instruction is important and can be effective. With respect to the second point, teachers need to be able to distinguish between the ability to use grammar effectively and the ability to describe it. Reaching a level of comfort with description is an important component of successful grammar instruction.

Form-Focused Instruction

For many years, grammar instruction held a prominent place in the L2 classroom (as seen in audiolingual and grammar translation methods of language teaching). In the 1970s and 1980s, the focus of instruction moved away from grammar teaching in favor of more communicative language teaching approaches that excluded grammar from classroom activities. More recently, grammar instruction has gained popularity as an effective way of helping adults gain (and retain) grammar knowledge, as long as it is incorporated into real communicative and meaningful language use. In the literature, this is known as *focus on form* or *form-focused instruction*, an approach to grammar learning that views meaning and communicative value as primary but also sees the need for specific grammar instruction so that learners' attention can be drawn to forms (Long, 1991). Research that synthesizes form-focused instruction (Ellis, 2002; Norris & Ortega, 2000) finds that form-focused instruction is effective in helping students develop grammar and, in some cases, can even help learners focus their attention on specific grammar structures that, through practice, can lead to implicit knowledge.

Form-focused instruction of grammar has advantages beyond research support for it. In many contexts, teachers may not be able to wait for certain grammar features to appear in communicative contexts. Students may avoid using a feature, or a feature may not be frequent enough to provide adequate practice. Addressing grammar explicitly provides students with focused practice so that they can use it more appropriately and accurately in higher stakes contexts such as academic papers or presentations. Teachers also face the decision of what grammar features to include in their instruction. The basic distinction that guides such decisions is whether they are choosing a grammar feature in a *reactive* way (i.e., providing instruction on a grammar feature that students are having trouble with) or a *proactive* way (i.e., making decisions on what grammar problems students may have and providing instruction prior to their use of the feature). Lively debates in form-focused instruction research concern issues such as whether reactive form-focused instruction is a truly communicatively meaningful activity and whether proactive decisions are less effective than reactive ones. Teachers, on the other hand, are more likely to adopt both proactive and reactive approaches to form-focused instruction.

REFLECTIVE QUESTION

● What factors are important in deciding whether to focus on grammar proactively or reactively?

In addition to the process of deciding what grammar forms to teach, teachers can focus on grammar in the L2 classroom in many different ways. A basic distinction in grammar instruction concerns the difference between activities that provide students with relevant examples of grammar forms (input) and activities in which students practice using grammar forms (output). As with the distinction between proactive and reactive approaches to form-focused instruction, researchers vary in their perspectives on the effectiveness of both input- and output-based approaches. Teachers, however, are likely to adopt both. An excellent overview of these two approaches is found in Nassaji and Fotos (2011) who describe six different options, three related to language input (processing instruction, textual enhancement, and discourse) and three related to interaction or language output (interactional feedback, structured grammar-focused tasks, and collaborative output tasks). The book includes a description of each alternative and helpful guidelines to follow for each of the options. In its final section, Nassaji and Fotos advocate for a multifaceted approach to form-focused instruction that adopts a range of options depending on factors related to teaching context and a teacher's level of comfort. This short discussion of the role of form-focused instruction illustrates the connection between research and pedagogy. Researchers are interested in looking at the effectiveness of specific approaches to form-focused instruction related to what forms to teach (proactive versus reactive) or by different approaches to teaching (input versus output). Teachers, on the other hand, are interested in helping their students use grammar more accurately, meaningfully and appropriately. In this sense, teachers should use research to inform their decisions about what and how to teach grammar but also keep in mind that the goal of a teacher is not to find "the best" or "most effective" way to teach grammar, but rather to make informed decisions based on the context and the student's needs. In this sense, teachers are more likely to benefit from understanding what factors (proactive/reactive; input/output) guide their decisions in a given context rather than identifying the "most effective" way to teach across contexts. This might seem obvious to many teachers, but keeping these pedagogical goals in mind is always good. The following chapter will address some basic guidelines for teaching grammar that will expand on the idea of choice and techniques.

REFLECTIVE QUESTION

- What types of grammar activities are you most comfortable using in class: input or output activities?

Implicit and Explicit Grammar Knowledge

Many highly proficient speakers of English may not be able to tell you why, but they do know that *I gave it up* is preferable over *I gave up it*. Highly proficient speakers are also more likely to use correct or appropriate grammar forms even if they cannot explain the rules that they successfully use in their daily production. On the other hand, many L2 learners at lower proficiency levels often do not possess the same type of knowledge; they may be able to explain a grammar rule but not use the rule appropriately. As discussed in chapter 1, this distinction between explicit and implicit knowledge is an important one for both teachers and students because no clear relationship exists between the ability to talk about grammar and the ability to use grammar. Grammar teachers must have some explicit knowledge of grammar to be able to respond to student output and provide adequate feedback and explanation to aid students in the development of grammar ability. The extent of this teacher knowledge, however, is subject to a good deal of variation. Furthermore, relying on too much explicit explanation of grammar can overburden (or perhaps even bore) students, so teachers need to learn to balance clear explanations with multiple opportunities to use language in meaningful ways. The goal of grammar teaching is not to teach grammar rules but to help students use language in accurate, meaningful, and appropriate ways. For students, having some explicit knowledge of grammar can help them to notice when and how certain grammar features are used or to see some mismatch between their knowledge of a given rule and their ability to use the rule in meaningful ways.

Even for teachers confident in talking about grammar, the corpus perspective covered in chapter 3 may challenge some of their intuitions about grammar form, meaning, and use. In one sense, whether teachers are, or are not, confident in their ability to talk about grammar with students, having reliable sources on how grammar is used in different contexts is invaluable. In another sense, though, the extent to which teachers are confident in their ability to talk about grammar will likely have an important impact on how they decide to teach it.

The implicit–explicit knowledge distinction is an important one for grammar teachers and leads to an interesting question: is it possible to teach grammar without being comfortable explaining it? Ultimately, individual teachers (and sometimes program administrators) must decide on the extent to which teachers need to have explicit knowledge of grammar to teach it. Explicit knowledge of grammar is sometimes covered in school subjects or in teacher-training programs, but not all programs stress its importance. Teachers may have very different levels of interest (or even ability) in explaining grammar. Although advocating for some level of comfort in describing grammar is wise, teachers need to decide the relevance of their explicit knowledge relative to a given grammar feature. If they view explicit knowledge as important, then the information provided in chapter 2 and resources such as those described in chapter 3 can help them gain explicit grammar knowledge.

Alternatively, teachers who do not feel comfortable in grammar description may still be effective grammar teachers if they acknowledge the extent of their current grammar knowledge and design tasks that do not require extensive explanation. For example, teachers can create activities that expose learners to using grammar forms or requires them to so do without discussing the grammar rules. The following chapter provides some guidelines for focusing on grammar that relate to FMU, corpus information, and the types of grammar knowledge of individual teachers.

CHAPTER 5

Issues in Grammar Teaching

This chapter discusses some concepts and guidelines relevant to the teaching of L2 learners in general and, in some cases, grammar in particular. The issues can guide teachers in the decisions they make when setting up syllabi or designing activities with a grammar focus. The topics addressed in this chapter are (1) teaching context and language background of teachers, (2) inductive and deductive instruction, (3) task-based language teaching, (4) addressing errors in the classroom, (5) choosing grammar features to teach, (6) assessing grammar ability, and (7) grammar teaching guidelines.

Teaching Context and Language Background of Teachers

Most teachers of English are aware of the distinction between English as a second language (ESL, teaching English in a country where English is the dominant language) and English as a foreign language (EFL, teaching English in a country where English is not a dominant language). Given the spread of English around the world and access to English language media via the internet, the traditional distinction between second or foreign language may not be as clear-cut.

Many places in the world outside of major English-speaking areas such as Great Britain, Canada, the United States, Australia, and New Zealand have native speakers of English (such as in India, Kenya, and Singapore). Additionally, even within a traditionally English-dominant country, English is not dominant in some places.

Despite the difficulty maintaining a strict ESL–EFL distinction, understanding the differences between the two contexts can be helpful for teachers. In an ESL context, the opportunities for interaction and exposure to English may be greater than in many EFL settings. EFL contexts may have more set curricula and larger class sizes than in ESL environments. Teachers should consider their context carefully when selecting activities. Some EFL settings may exert more pressure on teachers to locate and adapt materials for classroom use; in some ESL environments, teachers have greater access to a range of teaching materials as well as more opportunities for learners to interact with native speakers. Additionally, in many ESL contexts, students bring a variety of native language backgrounds, so the opportunities to interact in English maybe greater than in some EFL contexts where students not only share a native language but also share many cultural norms including those involving expectations for instruction.

The proficiency level of students is also an essential consideration. Lower-proficiency students need to master basic grammar concepts (e.g., subjects, predicates, objects, word forms, simple tenses) before moving on to more complex ones (e.g., agreement, perfect aspect, relative clauses). Introducing complex structures to students at lower proficiency can cause anxiety or result in a lack of motivation.

REFLECTIVE QUESTIONS

● How would you describe your current teaching context or a context in which you hope to teach? How might your context affect the way you address grammar in the classroom?

Another important factor in grammar teaching is the teacher's language background and experience. A teacher's ability to use research-based best practices and language teaching pedagogy, and their level of English language proficiency are more important than whether they have learned English as a first language or as an additional language. Teachers who have learned English as an additional language may have advantages, in that they may be more likely to have explicit knowledge of grammar, and can explain grammar to students more easily, while some native speakers may only rely on intuition. Teachers who have grown up in an English speaking environment, or with English as a native language, might have deeper cultural understandings, strong pronunciation, and fluency in using and understanding figurative expressions and communications with subtle or hidden meanings.

REFLECTIVE QUESTIONS

- What are some advantages of having learned English as an additional language? when teaching grammar?

- What are some advantages of being a native speaker or having been deeply immersed in an English speaking environment when teaching grammar?

While there are different advantages to having learned English as a native speaker or as an additional language, it is important to remember that strong language proficiency and proper teacher preparation are most important to effectively teaching grammar to English learners. The global status of English around the world provides many varieties of English that adopt norms that are completely appropriate in their given contexts. English language teachers need to consider the expectations of a given teaching context as well as their knowledge of subject matter. Grammar teachers who consider themselves native speakers should consider whether they have enough explicit knowledge of a grammar point before trying to teach it; grammar teachers who consider themselves nonnative speakers may need to find ways for students to use grammar features in communicative contexts and are not merely stating rules.

Inductive and Deductive Instruction

Grammar can be taught inductively or deductively. In an inductive approach, learners are guided through an activity with the goal of discovering grammar based on examples. By contrast, a deductive approach to language teaching provides explanations or discussions of rules prior to having students produce and practice the form. Consider this example activity:

Multi-words verbs

Read the following sentences. Discuss with your classmates what the underlined verb phrases mean.

    a. So you can see that his work doesn't really <u>fit in</u> anywhere specifically, but it <u>fits in</u> as a precursor to a lot of other things and the whole idea of painting those other images.

    b. That schedule of events is so long that it doesn't <u>fit in</u> those types of ads.

    c. Colin's been very happy over there and he has <u>fit in</u> like he never <u>fit in</u> in high school.

    d. Put them together and we'll see if they <u>fit in</u> the box.

Taking all the examples above into account, what does fit in mean? Does it always mean the same thing?

This inductive activity asks learners to discuss and decide on the meanings of the underlined multiword verb. No definition is provided, so students must instead determine meaning from the context or by interacting with a fellow classmate.

By contrast, a deductive approach to language teaching provides explanations or discussions of rules before students produce and practice. For example, a deductive approach to teaching multiword verbs would teach learners about the different types of multiword verbs (as outlined in chapter 3) and then include an activity that asks them to identify or produce different types of multiword verbs by reference to the rules provided.

REFLECTIVE QUESTIONS

● Think of some other examples of inductive or deductive grammar teaching. Do you prefer one approach to the other? What factors lead you toward one approach or the other?

Inductive approaches to grammar teaching, especially those that refer to corpora, are associated with data-driven learning (DDL), an approach to language teaching in which learners discover grammar rules by either directly interacting with corpora or with corpus information (Johns, 1991). A key component of DDL, along with the use of authentic data and an emphasis on learner autonomy, is that students uncover grammar rules through their exposure to language (induction).

Thornbury (1999) contrasts inductive and deductive activities by reference to how grammar teaching is organized in the classroom. Deductive grammar teaching follows a Presentation ➜ Practice ➜ Production organization, where a grammar point is first explained to the students (generally in the form of a rule). Afocused practice activity follows and then a freer productive activity. By contrast, inductive grammar teaching follows a Task ➜ Teach ➜ Task format, where students are first engaged in a communicative task designed to focus on a grammar structure (or in some cases, develop a rule from the provided examples). As a final step, students are given a task similar to (or in some cases, the same as) the original one.

REFLECTIVE QUESTION

● Try to devise an inductive and a deductive grammar activity using the same feature. Was one easier than the other to construct?

Task-Based Language Teaching

Teachers may often feel a tension between teaching students with reference to real communicative acts and providing opportunities to focus on specific grammar structures. As the previous chapter demonstrated, research supports form-focused instruction as long as learners engage in using the targeted form for a communicative purpose as opposed to a decontextualized activity that lacks meaning, communicative purpose, and context. To focus on form under these conditions, grammar tasks can be used.

A classroom task can be seen as anything that a student is asked to do in class. In this sense, asking students to choral read or go around the room and ask classmates to change two independent clauses into a subordinate and independent clause could all be considered tasks in the traditional sense of the word. More recently, task-based language teaching (TBLT), an approach to language that combines communicative language teaching with the use of authentic language used for a real purpose, has given the term *task* a different connotation in many teaching contexts (see Nunan, 2004, for an excellent illustration of designing and implementing tasks in the L2 classroom). In this more recent sense of the word, a task is a carefully designed activity that gets learners to use language to fulfill some specific function for some purpose.

Although TBLT proponents define and structure tasks differently, TBLT can be seen as having four major components:

1. The purpose of the task is to complete some objective or purpose. Most often the objective is decided by the teacher or materials developer, but there are cases in which the student(s) can decide on the objective.

2. Tasks are meaning based, not form based. Forms used during the task are not the focus of the activity; instead, the focus is on task completion.

3. The outcome of the task should not be open ended. Tasks need to have identifiable ending points so that learners are able to assess their performance in relation to the task.

4. Although it is possible to have students complete tasks individually, most often tasks are done in groups so that learners have a chance to interact in the target language.

Perhaps the best way to illustrate these aspects of TBLT is to look at a sample activity.

Task-Based Language Teaching Activity Detectives

Procedure: An object to be "stolen"—say, a coin or a ring—is decided on. One student (the "detective") is sent out of the room. One of the remaining students is given the object; he or she is the "thief." The detective returns and tries to find the thief by asking participants: *Do you have it?*

Each participant—including the actual thief—denies guilt and accuses someone else.

No, I don't have it. A has it! The detective turns to A with the same question and so on, until everyone has been asked and has denied responsibility. The detective then has to decide in three guesses who is lying—who "looks guilty." The process is then repeated with another detective and another thief.

Variations: The activity may be made more lively by encouraging students to act innocent or indignant as convincingly as they can: they may change the emphasis or intonation of the set sentences as they wish, add gestures, and so on. Another technique, which abandons verisimilitude but helps fluency, is to get the class to complete the round of "interrogations" as quickly as possible (*Let's see if we can get round the whole class in two minutes . . . Let's see if we can do it again in even less time*).

Source: Adapted from Ur (1988, pp. 123–124).

This activity is designed to elicit *have/has got* as a main verb (as opposed to a modal verb), but the objective of the activity is to find the thief, not to practice the grammar form (in this way it meets criteria #1). Although some language forms are provided (*Do you have it?*), the focus is not on form (criteria #2). Once the thief is uncovered, the activity is repeated with students playing different roles. For this reason, the activity is not open ended, which meets criteria #3. Finally, criteria #4 is satisfied because the students are interacting with one another to complete the task.

Learner Errors

Another essential consideration is how to deal with learner errors. This is especially true in grammar classes where there is often much focus on accuracy. Errors are a natural part of using language and may be considered appropriate in more informal (e.g., conversational) contexts. But to make grammar errors in other contexts (emails to professors, professional letters, and written assignments) is quite different. In these contexts, error-free grammar is expected.

Teachers have their grammar radar ready to detect errors in certain contexts and should consider applying this same concept to their own classrooms. Creating activities that do not focus on accurate production is one way to decrease a focus on errors. Small-group discussions that require learners to work toward completion of a task (such as presenting their findings or discussing outcomes with a larger group) allow students to focus more on content than on accuracy. In other activities (handing in a written assignment for grading), accurate production is expected. This is especially true when teachers construct a written assignment that has gone through the editing process so that learners can focus on the content in one or more drafts but then (through the help of the teacher or, in some cases, through peer editing) on grammar accuracy in a later draft.

REFLECTIVE QUESTIONS

- How do you address learner errors in a given class? Do you pay more attention to accuracy over meaningfulness and appropriacy?

- How does an FMU perspective on grammar relate to your view on learner errors?

Choosing Grammar Features

Teachers who use a reactive approach to the selection of grammar features are guided by student production, as the grammar being taught relates directly to grammar features with which the students are having trouble. In a proactive approach, a number of factors can guide teachers in their choice of features. If the teaching context allows teachers flexibility in feature selection, they should make their proactive decisions with respect to the needs of their learners. For example, in teaching contexts with an academic focus, teaching different ways of hedging is useful. Modals of possibility such as *might* or *could* or verbs such as *suggest* or *seems* are useful structures in most types of academic writing. If the class is for new immigrants to an English-speaking country, it likely focuses on functions such as asking for directions (e.g., *Could you please tell me where the post office is?*) and successfully completing service encounters, such as going to the bank (e.g., *I would like to make a deposit*).

Teachers should also use meaning and information to guide their selection of grammar features. Grammar points based purely on form (such as third-person agreement or, in some cases, article use) are not as important as those aspects of grammar that interfere with meaning or use—for example, using an imperative in a service encounter where a more polite form is expected. In such a case, *Give me a cup of coffee* is less appropriate than *Would you please give me a cup of coffee?*

A good argument can be made to focus on the most common patterns or words associated with a given structure (see chapter 3 for examples). Reference books such as the LGSWE are useful resources. As described in chapter 3, publicly available corpora can provide frequency information with very little effort. Thus, corpus information can help teachers understand how particular structures work in English (related to teacher knowledge of grammar) and also guide teachers in their presentation of materials and selection of features (teaching knowledge of grammar).

In addition to choosing frequent relevant features and focusing on meaning and use, teachers should also reach a level of comfort in their explicit knowledge of grammar. This can be done by taking a grammar course or by keeping a few steps ahead of the students by studying the grammar and practicing explanations before class.

REFLECTIVE QUESTION

● In addition to the factors described above, what others might guide your choice of grammar features to cover in your instruction?

Assessing Grammar

As Ur (1988) reminds teachers, "[w]e have to know where we are to know where to go next" (p. 10). To understand if students are able to use grammar effectively, teachers must assess their grammar ability. Ways of doing so can raise complicated issues related to reliability and construct validity (Purpura, 2004), but the purpose of this section is to provide teachers with some useful ways of looking at grammar assessment in the classroom. Two main concepts related to assessment are covered: (1) assessing FMU and (2) discrete item versus holistic assessment.

Just as grammar is defined from an FMU perspective, teachers should find ways of assessing grammar to include all three aspects. Evaluating form (generally through reference to accuracy) is perhaps what most teachers (and students) focus on in grammar assessments. For example, formal knowledge can be assessed in sentence completion tasks. Often these tasks ask students to complete sentences such as *I will call you before I _____*. Alternatively, teachers may ask students to write sentences using particular words or structures. The following example asks students to write sentences using four-word lexical bundles.

Lexical Bundle Activity

Use the following groups of words to write a sentence.
You may not change the form of any of the words.

are you going to　　　　　　*is going to be*

one of the things　　　　　　*I don't want to*

This activity uses some of the frequent lexical bundles shown in Table 3.4 (in chapter 3) and assesses the ability to incorporate the bundles into grammatical sentences, an indication of formal knowledge. As discussed in chapter 3, lexical bundles incorporate fragments of phrases and clauses so teachers can choose bundles with particular structures depending on the focus of the class.

In addition to form, meaning can also be assessed in the grammar classroom. For example, students can be asked illustrate their knowledge of the past perfect by selecting a sentence with a similar meaning.

Meaning Activity

Choose the sentence (A, B, or C) that has the same meaning as the following sentence:

Lizzy hadn't been to the party before Tom left.

    A. Tom came to the party early.

    B. Tom and Lizzy were at the party together.

    C. Lizzy came to the party and didn't see Tom.

Knowledge of grammar use can be determined by having students complete discourse completion tasks such as the following:

Discourse Completion Activity

You need to miss class next week because of an important appointment. How would you ask your teacher for permission?

These are just examples of assessing FMU. For teachers interested in other ways of assessing these three aspects of grammar, *The Grammar Book* (Celce-Murcia & Larsen-Freeman, 2015) is a good place to start. Although the specifics of the activity type are best left to teachers (or to books with a focus different from this one), teachers and students can benefit from an approach to grammar that does not only relate to formal knowledge. Finding ways of assessing meaning and use helps teachers and learners to gain a wider perspective on grammar and how to use it for communicative purposes.

In addition to FMU, teachers must also decide whether to focus on discrete items (such as those just described) or take a more holistic approach in assessing grammar. Discrete testing allows more control over the aspects of grammar being assessed, but teachers run the risk of assessing students in noncommunicative or nonauthentic situations.

Holistic grammar assessment can come in the form of speaking (an oral interview or presentation) or in writing (from a prompt, for example).

Teachers can then give a general accuracy score, or they may choose to consider other factors such as complexity or range of grammar structures as well as appropriate use of language conventions. The advantage of the more holistic approach is that students are using language for a more authentic purpose than what is often found in discrete-item measures. Teachers may choose to use holistic activities to identify grammar features that will be the focus of subsequent lessons. On the other hand, holistic grammar measures may not elicit targeted grammar structures because of avoidance or other strategies employed by students.

REFLECTIVE QUESTIONS

- In your current teaching context, how might you address meaning and use aspects of grammar?

- Do you prefer a discrete-item or a holistic approach?

Guidelines for Grammar Teaching

In a very useful chapter for teachers, Richards and Reppen (2016) provide 12 principles of grammar instruction and, for some principles, offer sample activities. Each of these will be discussed in relation to ideas already covered in this book.

1. Identify the Grammar Resources that Students Need

As noted, different contexts require different resources because the grammar needs of students depend on the grammar that is used or expected in a given context, assignment, or task. For example, a narrative task (whether written or spoken) requires students to have some control over the tense and aspect of verbs because tasks of this type require events to relate to each other in some sequence. From an FMU perspective, the forms of verbs used in narratives need to express various meanings related to a sequence of events; these forms fulfill this requirement of narratives. Note that this particular perspective on grammar resources is proactive in that the teacher makes *a priori* decisions on the grammar needed to complete the task. Alternatively, if accurate production is expected, some reactive instruction may be required once students are producing narrative to address this expectation.

2. Teach Awareness of the Nature of Texts

An awareness of the grammar features in texts relates to the role of explicit knowledge of grammar and how various types of texts use it. One advantage of considering text awareness relates to the co-occurrence of linguistic features in texts. Academic writing, for example, employs many different grammar features that make noun phrases longer (attributive adjectives, prepositional phrases following nouns, and relative clauses). Raising awareness of these features in texts not only shows students examples of these specific features, but also illustrates how they are often found together in the same sentence or text.

3. Develop Awareness of the Difference Between Written and Spoken Language

Similar to number 2, awareness relates to explicit knowledge. As has been consistently illustrated through corpus analyses, written and spoken language are quite different in their grammar characteristics. An awareness of these differences, and perhaps even potential reasons for these differences, can help students to understand not only what differs between written and spoken language but also why these differences exist. For example, because writing is constructed in one place for a reader in another place, the lack of shared space necessitates grammar that establishes clear reference. In spoken language where the participants share the same physical space, speakers are more likely to use pronouns such as *this, that, it* to refer to things, ideas, or concepts because an opportunity exists for the participants to clarify any unclear reference or to actually note pronoun referents in a shared space.

4. Use Corpora to Explore Texts

Chapter 3 illustrates how teachers can use corpora to access reliable and authentic information about form, meaning, and use. As noted in chapter 4, corpora can also be used in the classroom to raise awareness of grammar through deductive and inductive instruction. The use of corpora to raise awareness of grammar in both teachers and students permits a wide and reliable resource to raise an FMU perspective on grammar and allows both teachers and students to actively participate in promoting accurate, meaningful, and appropriate language use.

5. Use a Variety of Teaching Approaches

The need to incorporate multiple approaches has been mentioned through-out this book. Whether taking an inductive or a deductive approach or stressing input or output, effective form-focused instruction should not rely on a single approach or technique. The goal of grammar teaching is to foster accurate, meaningful, and appropriate use of language in a variety of contexts and for a variety of purposes. A single approach to grammar instruction will not foster such a goal.

6. Provide Opportunities for Guided Noticing

The concept of noticing relates to input perspectives on language develop-ment. Of all the potential input to which students are exposed, the parts that they are able to notice have a strong impact on their language development. With its potential to inform students' explicit knowledge of a given feature or set of features, form-focused instruction is one way to lead students to observe grammar features. Of course, not all learning happens through explicit instruction—students can learn much more than what they are taught—but the type of guided noticing facilitated through grammar instruction is an important component in its success.

7. Provide Opportunities for Meaningful Communicative Practice

Practice is, by definition, an output activity, but, as discussed in previous chapters, the output practice should not be purely mechanical. The FMU perspective on grammar adopted in this book stresses the relevance of these three aspects of grammar. Using grammar practice activities that stress both the meaning of a grammar form as well as how to use it in communicative situations should be a goal of grammar teaching.

8. Provide Opportunities for Students to Produce Stretched Output

The importance of stretched output relates to providing activities that challenge learners to produce language they modify from something they produced earlier. In this sense, students have the opportunity to expand on their ideas, which also necessitates the use of a wider range of grammar features. This can be achieved by redrafting a previously written assignment, answering questions on a presentation, or completing a related (but more complex) assignment that follows from an easier assignment.

9. Make Links Between Grammar and Vocabulary

Separating grammar and vocabulary can be difficult. As noted in chapter 3, some aspects of grammar (e.g., multiword verbs) are actually vocabulary items. Additionally, even though the lexical bundles discussed in chapter 3 are groups of words, they have a cohesive meaning because they fulfill specific functional purposes in a text. Illustrating how specific types of words determine grammar functions (e.g., whether a verb is transitive or intransitive) also shows how specific words carry grammatical meaning. Teachers should be prepared to make these distinctions clear to students and promote the idea that knowing a word includes knowing how the word is used in a sentence (which necessitates grammar knowledge).

10. Use Student Errors to Inform Instruction

This issue has been discussed in relation to the role of reactive form-focused instruction. Providing grammar instruction on actual student errors not only provides input that students may more likely notice, but also helps students present their own ideas with greater control of accuracy.

11. Integrate Grammar with the Four Skills

Although some teachers may still use decontextualized grammar instruction, the importance of meaningful communicative activities necessitates the use of grammar as it relates to the four skills of reading, writing, speaking, and listening. Furthermore, more than one skill can also be used to promote grammar instruction (listening to write; reading to write).

12. Use Resources of the Internet and Technology

The internet can provide rich input for students and can also offer opportunities for interaction with other users of English. This can, of course be done with both writing and speaking. Meaningful input and output activities are readily available, and teachers should be aware of the opportunities available to students. Sometimes students can be the best resource to identify useful technology that promotes language use, but numerous resources are available for teachers who do a simple internet search.

REFLECTIVE QUESTION

● Can you think of other components not mentioned here that are also important in your teaching context?

This chapter ends with a sample lesson that covers form, meaning, and use activities about the differences between *since* and *for*. Each activity could be used as a separate activity or could be sequenced into a single lesson.

Sample lesson: Using *Since and For* to Express Time

This lesson would take place after the students had already discussed the present perfect in class. It is for upper intermediate to advanced students.

Activity 1: Meaning Activity

Write or project the following sentences. Highlight the words *since* and *for* to make them more salient.

● *Yuhki Yamashita's team has been using the beta version of Coda since July.*

● *That may be difficult for the nonprofit, which hasn't raised more than $50,000 a year since at least 2007.*

● *The university has been without a chief diversity officer for about a year.*

● *David and I have been doing this for over 20 years.*

Ask students to decide how *since* and *for* are used differently.

Once they have tried to guess how they are used, draw a simple timeline on the board.

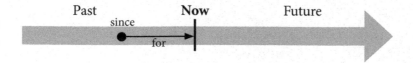

- *Since* tells us when something started.
- *For* describes a process to say how long something lasted in a period of time that has a beginning and an end.

Write or project these sentences on the board, and ask students to decide between *since* or *for*:

- *I have worked there _____ three years.*
- *I have worked there _____ April.*

Ask students to draw a timeline of the two sentences that shows the difference between *since* and *for*.

I've worked there for three years.

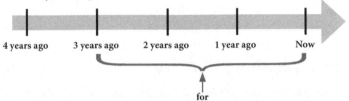

I've worked there since April.

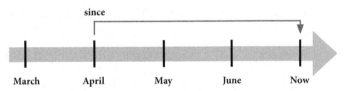

Activity 2: Meaning Activity

Show students the sentence *Today is Thursday. Alexander has been in Dubai since Sunday morning.* Ask one of the students to read the sentence, then ask the class the following questions:

- *When did Alexander arrive in Dubai?*
- *What was his first day in Dubai?*
- *What day is it today?*
- *How many days has Alexander been in Dubai?*

Have students finish the sentence: *Alexander has been in Dubai for _____ days.*

Activity 3: Meaning and Use Activity

Have students work together to present answers to the following questions.

- Explain why the authors used *since* and *for* in the same sentence:

  Jurors will return for a fifth day of work Friday. They've been at it for nearly 40 hours since getting the case Monday.

  Peter stared at the screen on his desk, which he had been doing since early that morning, and for the past five days.

- What does *it* refer to in the following sentence? Why did the author use *since*?

  *Judges have not paid much attention to Koistinen in recent times. Indeed, it has been more than a decade since **it** was last cited in a case.*

Activity 4: Meaning Activity

Provide students with the following time adverbials, and ask them to choose between *since* and *for*. They need to justify their decision and relate it to the rule previously discussed about the difference between *since* and *for*.

1. *ten minutes*
2. *Christmas*
3. *1966*
4. *10 o'clock*
5. *last night*
7. *three years*
9. *August*
11. *winter*
6. *a lifetime*
8. *a week*
10. *last week*
12. *I was 6*

Activity 5: Form and Meaning Activity: Placement of Phrases with since/for

Show students that sometimes a phrase using *since* or *for* can be in different places in a sentence. For example,

__Since 1980__, the city of St. Louis lost another 6 percent of its population.

The city of St. Louis lost another 6 percent of its population __since 1980__.

Have students decide if it is possible to move the bolded phrases to different parts of the sentence in the following four examples.

*Another woman I know was so sick she had to stay in bed **for three months**.*

*The next day I commenced my search. **For three months** I continued it.*

*I have had nothing to eat **since yesterday** morning.*

***Since last year** when the embargo was lifted, we in Vietnam are better off in resolving the MIA issue because we were able to go out to talk to farmers.*

Is there some rule or principle that determines if the phrases can move?

REFLECTIVE QUESTIONS

- How does the previous lesson abide by the 12 principles of grammar instruction outlined in this chapter?

- What other activities could you use to include other principles?

CHAPTER 6

Conclusion

In some ways, all L2 teachers are grammar teachers because grammar is a constant component in both productive and receptive skills. Thus, all teachers need to have an understanding of grammar to be effective. But teaching grammar as its own subject also has a place. Recent research supports focusing on grammar in a communicatively meaningful way. Describing grammar from an FMU perspective allows teachers to see how meaning and context relate to grammar form. Such a view of grammar is useful for teachers because it provides a framework for understanding it from multiple perspectives. This, in turn, promotes student learning of grammar because it allows students to actively participate in their understanding and in their development toward accurate, appropriate, and meaningful language use.

In addition to FMU, reference to authentic language use bolsters grammar knowledge and teaching decisions by drawing from empirical descriptions of language use found in corpus-based grammars and publicly available corpora. Specifically, teachers can use frequency and register information to focus on the language students are most likely to encounter and be expected to produce in a given context (e.g., academic English or conversational English). This book has also demonstrated how a corpus perspective on grammar can aid teachers in their decisions about what grammar features to choose and what examples to use in their instruction.

As with FMU, the benefits relate not only to the selection of grammar features, but also to an understanding of grammar that allows teachers to explain it to students.

Reflective practice is an important component of teaching because it allows teachers to collect information about their knowledge of grammar, to examine their beliefs about how to teach grammar to learners, and to apply their acquired knowledge in individual instructional contexts and thereby increase their effectiveness. As with any subject, knowledge of subject matter and knowledge about effective teaching guide effective teachers. Reflective practice provides opportunities for teachers to remind themselves of why they teach and how they can teach most effectively.

Finally, reflective practice is an excellent way to raise awareness of the dynamism of language teaching. Just as learners take different paths toward language development, teachers should be constantly evolving as their knowledge of their subject evolves. As teachers gain experience in teaching knowledge, the approaches they use in grammar classes are also likely to develop and change over time. The same idea also relates to teacher knowledge. As knowledge of grammar form, meaning, and use progresses, so do the ways that teachers can think about grammar to improve instruction. In this sense, reflective practice is an excellent way to promote teacher development from both a teaching knowledge and a teacher knowledge perspective. Being open to change and improvement is an integral part of teacher development, and reflective practice can promote such growth in both experienced and inexperienced teachers.

References

Biber, D. (1988). *Variation across speech and writing.* Cambridge, England: Cambridge University Press.

Biber, D., & Conrad, S. (2019). *Register, genre, and style.* Cambridge, England: Cambridge University Press.

Biber, D., Conrad, S., & Cortes, V. (2004). If you look at . . . : lexical bundles in university teaching and textbooks. *Applied Linguistics, 25,* 371–405.

Biber, D., Johansson, S., Leech, G., Conrad, S., & Finegan, E. (1999). *Longman grammar of spoken and written English.* London, England: Longman.

Celce-Murcia, M., & Larsen-Freeman, D. (2015). *The grammar book: An ESL/EFL teacher's course* (3rd ed.). Boston, MA: Heinle & Heinle.

Davies, M. (2008). *The Corpus of Contemporary American English: 450 million words, 1990–present.* Retrieved from http://corpus.byu.edu/coca/.

Ellis, R. (2002). Does form-focused instruction affect the acquisition of implicit knowledge? A review of the research. *Studies in Second Language Acquisition, 24,* 223–236.

Ellis, R., Loewen, S., Elder, C., Reinders, H., Erla, R, & Philp, J. (Eds.). (2009). Implicit and Explicit Knowledge in Second Language Learning, Testing and Teaching. Bristol, England: Multilingual Matters.

Johns, T. (1991). Should you be persuaded: Two samples of data-driven learning materials. In T. Johns & P. King (Eds.), *Classroom concordancing* (pp.1–13). Birmingham, England: Centre for English Language Studies.

Larsen-Freeman, D. (2003). *Teaching language:From grammar to grammaring.* Boston, MA: Heinle & Heinle.

Long, M. (1991). Focus on form: A design feature in language teaching methodology. In K. DeBot, R. Ginsberg, & C. Kramsch (Eds.), *Foreign language research in cross-cultural perspective* (pp. 39–52). Amsterdam, The Netherlands: John Benjamins.

McCarthy, M., McCarten, J., & Sandiford, H. (2005). *Touchstone 1–4: From corpus to course book.* Cambridge, England: Cambridge University Press.

McEnery, T., Xiao, R., & Tono, Y. (2006). *Corpus-based language studies: An advanced resource book.* New York, NY: Routledge.

Nassaji, H., & Fotos, S. (2011). *Teaching grammar in second language classrooms: Integrating form-focused instruction in communicative context.* New York, NY: Routledge.

Norris, J., & Ortega, L. (2000). Effectiveness of L2 instruction: A research synthesis and quantitative meta-analysis. *Language Learning, 50,* 417–528.

Nunan, D. (2004). *Task-based language teaching.* Cambridge, England: Cambridge University Press.

Purpura, J. (2004). *Assessing grammar.* Cambridge, England: Cambridge University Press.

Reppen, R. (2012). *Grammar and beyond.* Cambridge, England: Cambridge University Press.

Richards, J. C., & Reppen, R. (2016). 12 principles of grammar instruction. In E. Hinkle (Ed.), *Teaching English grammar to speakers of other languages* (pp. 151–170). New York, NY: Routledge.

Thornbury, S. (1999). *How to teach grammar.* Essex, England: Longman.

Ur, P. (1988). *Grammar practice activities: A practical guide for teachers.*